ISBN 978-1-331-31659-6
PIBN 10173386

1 MONTH OF FREE READING

at

www.ForgottenBooks.com

By purchasing this book you are eligible for one month membership to ForgottenBooks.com, giving you unlimited access to our entire collection of over 700,000 titles via our web site and mobile apps.

To claim your free month visit:

www.forgottenbooks.com/free173386

Similar Books Are Available from
www.forgottenbooks.com

ted Ju...
...83
...1842

D. I. Rec.º 10 July. 184

THE SABBA

A POEM.

ˇ Bigelow

A POEM

IN TWO PARTS

BY ABIJAH BIGELOW

And he said unto them, The Sabbath was made for man, and not man for th Sabbath.
Therefore the Son of man is Lord also of the Sabbath.   Mark ii. 27, 28.
Search the Scriptures; for in them ye think ye have eternal life; and the are they which testify of me.   John v. 39.

WORCESTER:
PRINTED BY HENRY J. HOWLAND.
1842.

PREFACE.

To the sincere, pious, penitent Christian, the Sabbath is a holy and a blessed day. Oppressed by the cares, toils and duties of the week, the Sabbath comes to his relief, like as a spring of water to the refreshment of a thirsty traveller, in his journey through a dry and desert land. It reminds him of duties higher and holier than those of laboring for the honor and riches of this world. And while it reminds him that the period of his existence on earth is short, it reminds him also of a never ending existence beyond the grave. It reminds him that he is "fearfully and wonderfully made," that he is the creature of an invisible Creator, to whom he is indebted for his life, and for all the wonderful physical, moral and intellectual faculties with which he is endowed. It affords him a fit season "to look through nature up to nature's God," to contemplate his infinite perfections, and to admire the wisdom and goodness which has given him an habitation so exactly adapted to his capacities and wants. And what is of yet greater importance, it affords him an opportunity to read and reflect upon the revelation of God to man, that revelation which discloses the character of his Creator, his own character, the duties required of him in this life, and what he must do to inherit a life of immortality and blessedness in that world of spirits into which his soul must soon take its flight.

And will any one who duly estimates the value of his immortal soul, think one day in seven too great a portion of his time to devote to a preparation so important?

Considerations, like these, have deeply impressed upon my mind, the wisdom of the institution of the Sabbath, even upon the supposition that the institution was an ordinance of man, and not of God. But when we believe that "the Sabbath was made for man," by his allwise and beneficent Creator, and that it is an institution peculiarly calculated to promote his temporal and eternal happiness, how can we justify, or even excuse a wanton, or wilful neglect to observe it?

Frequent reflections upon the subject have convinced me of its immense importance, not only to individual, but to national happiness, and I was thus led to inquire into the causes which have induced so many, in this professedly Christian land, not only to neglect, but even treat it with contempt. The result of these reflections and inquiries I have attempted to embody in verse, instead of prose, hoping in that way to make a more permanent impression, upon the mind of the reader, of the truths intended to be inculcated. I have endeavored to advance no sentiments unsupported by history, reason, or revelation.

Pure religion, by which I mean Christianity, as revealed to us by Christ and his apostles, and a pious observance of the Sabbath, appear to me to be so intimately connected, that neither can long exist in a community, independent of the other. Where infidelity and irreligion abound, the Sabbath will not be observed, and where the Sabbath is not observed as a holy day, there will be little, or no religion.

Various causes have operated to undermine, in the minds of many, a belief in, and respect for, the Christian

Sabbath, and as a necessary consequence, a disregard of of it, as a holy day. Among these have been the bigotry, by which I mean the religious tyranny and intolerance, of many professed Christians, who for selfish and ambitious purposes have claimed and usurped the right to compel men, by force, to adopt particular creeds and forms of worship. These claims, rendered more obnoxious, by the selfish, and too often dissolute lives of such arrogant pretenders to infallibility, have been seized upon by infidels, alike selfish, ambitious and profligate, as a sufficient ground openly to denounce the Christian religion, as the work of artful men, designed to impose upon, and tyrannize over, their fellow men. In this way many, very many, without inquiry into the truths of Christianity, the purity of its doctrines and precepts, the free spirit which it breathes, and its repeated denunciations of all such ungodly professors, have been led to disbelieve and treat it with neglect and hatred.

I have, therefore, attempted to show, that bigots and infidels are each actuated by the same selfish motives, each alike hostile to true religion, the former seeking to oppress mankind under the sanction of religion, the latter, by boldly denouncing all religion as founded in priestcraft and superstition. It has been my desire to expose the errors and crimes of both, and to place religion upon its true ground, its own intrinsic excellence.

As every man should be able to give a reason for his faith, an attempt has been made to adduce some of the most plain and obvious facts and arguments, in support of the Bible, as a revelation from God to man. To the educated and enlightened Christain, these will not be new, but to many inquirers after truth they may be useful, so far, at least, as a guide to direct them to other and better sources of information. Should it have this effect, should

1*

it lead any to seek for a blessed immortality through him who came into the world to bring " life and immortality to light," and who was himself " the way and the truth and the life," my object will be accomplished, and my labor, however imperfect the work may be, as a poetic production, will not have been wholly useless.

A. BIGELOW

Worcester, March 9th, 1842.

THE SABBATH.

PART I.

Why, when old age has damp'd the fire,
That should poetic strains inspire,
Should I, whose mind in former years
Was burdened with continual cares,
Attempt grave truths in verse t'express, ⎱
With faint assurance that success, ⎰
Will my well meant intentions bless?
  'Tis not to sing a warrior's praise,
Or love for martial fame to raise;
'Tis not o'er daring crimes to throw,
A robe of glory, a false show
Of greatness, making vice appear,
More splendid, fascinating, fair,
Than modest virtue, moral worth,
Clad in the sober garb of truth:
Tis not on sceptic wings to soar,
To find a new creating pow'r,
Or new religion to devise,
Than Christ's more holy, or more wise,
That bids me rouse my feeble pow'rs,
In these my last, few leisure hours.
A theme more holy shall engage
The remnant of declining age.
  The Sabbath, sanctified and blest,
For man ordain'd a day of rest,
A day his Maker to adore,
A day his mercy to implore,

A day that should his heart impress
With his own need of holiness;
This day, so worthy his esteem,
And his regard, shall be my theme.
   Lord of the Sabbath to my heart,
Thy spirit and thy grace impart,
Inspire my thoughts, teach me thy foes,
With truths resistless to oppose.
O, aid me, in the minds of youth,
To engraft this all important truth,
That God the Sabbath day design'd,
To benefit and bless mankind,
That to observe it with delight,
With spirits humble and contrite,
Is the foundation strong and sure,
That will the storms of life endure,
Heaven and immortal bliss secure.
   Why was for man the Sabbath made?
Was wisdom in the law display'd,
Which order'd that the day should be
From worldly care and toil kept free?
And who is man?   Who gave him birth
Who made him tenant of the earth,
So well adapted to produce,
All things convenient for his use?
   With eyes intelligent behold,
The wondrous works the heavens unfold;
The sun, by day, dispensing light,
The silver moon, so fair and bright,
Planets and stars adorning night,
Each, by a Pow'r unseen, sustain'd,
Each, in the course, that Pow'r ordain'd
Revolving, all from countless years,
Moving in their appointed spheres,
So constant, so exact, so true,
That men their speed and orbits know.
In that almighty power, which plann'd
And formed the heavens, so vast and grand,
Behold the God, who gave man birth
And made him Lord o'er all on earth.

And does not man obedience owe ?
And is not his allegiance due,
To that almighty Pow'r whose will
His body form'd with perfect skill,
And all its diff'rent parts combin'd,
To act subservient to a mind,
In close, mysterious union join'd ?
  Ages have past, have roll'd away,
Since that sublime, terrific day,
When, veil'd in clouds, in fire and smoke,
God from the mount of Sinai spoke,
That man, although he might not see
The all creating Deity,
His voice and his commands might hear,
And Him, alone, adore and fear.
To man the Almighty there reveal'd
His moral law, yet unrepeal'd,
A law most just, most wisely given,
His rule for life, his guide to Heaven.
  Hear then, O, man, thy Lord's decree,
" Remember thou, the Sabbath day."
Rest from the labor, pause, reflect,
Thy duty learn, thy heart inspect,
To God your thoughts devoutly raise,
Let prayer, and gratitude, and praise,
Ascend to Him, who kindly hears,
As well the child's, as seraph's prayers.
  And who are they, who do not love,
Delight in, hallow and improve
The Sabbath day?   Let truth declare,
Nor small, nor great offenders spare.
  Oft have I seen the active boy,
His parents hope, his parents joy,
Allow'd to spend the Sabbath day,
In idle sports, or vicious play,
Allow'd with truant boys to roam,
O'er fields and woodlands far from home,
In search of pleasure, till his mind,
To wisdom, truth and duty blind,
Gave way to vice.   Thus seeds are found,

Though early sown, on fertile ground,
Neglected left, to sprout and die,
While noxious plants their place supply.
Soon, a small trespass as he strays,
With those more vers'd in mischief's ways,
Becomes the first, the fatal source,
Of his abandon'd, godless course.
To shun detection, and conceal
The fault he trembles to reveal,
Falsehood comes next, the lie is told,
With manners impudent and bold.
To this a petty theft succeeds,
Follow'd by more atrocious deeds.
Suspected, watch'd, the boy is caught,
Before the bar of justice brought.
His trial comes.   In vain he pleads,
Not guilty of the atrocious deeds
Laid to his charge.   In vain he tries,
By doubts to blind the Jurors' eyes.
The evidence adduced is plain,
No doubts the Jurors entertain.
All in the Verdict are agreed,
The record of his guilt is made,
The Court his punishment award ⎫
Imprisonment and labor hard, ⎬
The public from like crimes to guard, ⎭
Him to reform, to let all know,
Transgression is the road to woe.
Alas, for her, the afflicted one,
The mother of the yet loved son,
Daily and nightly she doth weep,
Distressing dreams disturb her sleep,
Her grief, which no bright hopes allay,
Fast wear her strength and life away.
Oft she laments her past neglect,
To teach, when young, her son to respect
The Sabbath day. " Had he in youth,
" Been taught," she cries, " the words of truth,
' Been taught his God to love, to mind
" His laws adapted and design'd

" Youth to instruct, train up, direct,
" And from temptation's snares protect,
" I had not now beheld my son,
" For crimes condemn'd, disgrac'd, undone,
" Nor had I now been left to mourn,
" That unto me a son was born,
" To pierce, as with a poison'd dart,
" My ever anxious, doting heart,
" With wound incurable, with grief,
" Too deep infix'd to find relief."
   Nor does a mother mourn alone,
The fall and ruin of a son.
Grief breaks an aged Father's rest,
Deep anguish fills a sister's breast.
" O, what disgrace," they cry, " what shame
" The boy has brought upon our name,
" And what, alas, will be his doom,
" His sentence in the world to come ?"
How lamentable tis to see
Deluded youth thus early stray
From virtue's path, from that straight road
Which leads to duty and to God.
   But why expect that thoughtless youth,
Untaught to love the words of truth,
Untrain'd when young, what way to go,
Should not a vicious course pursue ?
Their crimes, indeed, should be restrain'd,
The law, by punishments, maintain'd.
But O, if human laws could reach
The greater criminals who teach
Doctrines corrupt, which undermine
All love, in youth, for truths divine,
To these would punishment belong,
As guilty of the greater wrong.
   These are the men, who cannot brook
The doctrines of the sacred book.
Their haughty souls cannot endure
The law of God, it is too pure.
The law reveal'd, to be man's guide,
Suits not their vanity and pride.

Its strict requirements, precepts, rules,
So war with their unhumbled souls,
They hate it, hate its truths to hear,
Deny, but still, its truths they fear.
　As that arch fiend, man's first great foe,
By guile, fill'd earth with sin and woe,
So they, alike corrupt and base,
Disdain their Maker's proffer'd grace,
Yea, rather than submit, prefer
With Heaven to wage rebellious war;
Delighted to seduce, degrade,
And ruin youth, their cause to aid.
　The bias of the youthful mind,
To rise above restraint inclin'd,
With pleasure clings to every plea
Which seems to give it liberty
T' indulge in all the vain desires,
A reckless love of sport inspires.
This nat'ral bias is the snare,
Which reckless infidels prepare,
To tempt the young, then, as they stray,
In pleasure's fascinating way,
Their course applaud, and thus with skill,
Their poisonous principles instil.
　" Would you be great, then boldly dare
" Shake off all superstitious fear,
" Let not religious shackles bind
" The freedom of a freeborn mind.
" Modern philosophers grown wise,
" The Bible term a book of lies,
" A trick of State, a forgery,
" Weak minds to frighten, terrify,
" To keep in awe of Priests and knaves,
" And make them more obedient slaves.
" This life, they say, bounds man's career,
" So taught a Hume, so taught Voltaire,
" And so teach all, whose minds are free,
" From foolish fears and bigotry."
　Such is the language, such the art,
Us'd to corrupt the youthful heart,

By infidels, who boldly claim,
That truth and freedom is their aim.
　Christians profess'd, alas, 'tis true,
Too often by their actions show,
And by their worldly spirit prove,
Self, not Christianity, they love.
　But what if knaves assume the dress,
Of Christian faith and holiness?
What if proud bigots boldly dare,
Their own, as God's decrees, declare?
And hypocrites would Christians seem,
To court preferment, or esteem?
What does it prove, but this sad fact,
That villains will, like villains act?
　O, would to Heaven that I could tear,
From such false hearts, the mask they wear,
That hypocrites no more might claim
A right to bear the Christian name,
Or pure religion ever be
Identified with bigotry.
　But shall religion be abus'd,
Because by wicked men misus'd?
Shall men of fire the use deny,
Because some base incend'ary,
May, and oft does, its aid employ,
Their habitations to destroy?
The traitor to effect his end,
Assumes the language of a friend,
And men, most wicked, oft are found,
Mere self, their aim, on Christian ground.
　Such, since the day, when God's own Son,
Descended from his Father's throne,
The Messenger of love and grace,
To Adam's sin polluted race,
Have sought, as ministers of God,
O'er man to wield a tyrant's rod,
To form his creed, demand his faith,
By no less penalty than death.
　Thus Rome's proud Pontiffs claim'd to rule,
The Church of Christ without control,

Priests to denounce, Kings to dethrone,
Who dar'd their lofty claims disown,
Yet ready to uphold and aid
All who to them their homage paid.
Hence Kings and Priests with Popes combin'd
To overawe the human mind.
At length, a nobler spirit rose,
Their deeds unholy t' expose;
A spirit, unsubdued by fear,
Of threats, or punishments severe,
Which, with the Bible for its guide,
Their bold anathemas defied,
Their practices corrupt assailed,
And to the world their crimes unveil'd.
Still Popes and Kings their claims maintain'd,
Their hands with blood of millions stain'd,
Resolv'd, however wrong, their power,
By force, or terror, to secure.
  Of their inhuman deeds, a few
Will prove, most clearly, how untrue,
How base and arrogant their claim,
Their right t' assume the Christian name.
  When Philip second, son and heir,
Of that distinguish'd man of war,
Charles, call'd the Great, and great he was,
If disregard of human laws,
If battles won, by thousands slain,
To add new States to his domain,
Be great; but if mankind to bless,
And add to human happiness,
Make monarchs great, Charles had no claim,
No right, or title, to the name.
When Philip, like the haughty son,
Of that fam'd King, wise Solomon,
From Charles his vast dominions took,
He harder made the people's yoke.
Resolv'd, with pow'r supreme, to reign,
His will in Church and State maintain.
The Inquisition's pow'r he made
His own intolerance to aid.

A pow'r, on whomsoe'r it please,
Without complaint, or oath to seize,
And them imprison, torture, try,
On bare assertion of a spy,
A venal spy, and sure to be,
A knave, or bitter enemy,
And them in dungeons dark enchain,
As prisoners there for life detain,
Or else, strange sacrifice for faith,
Expose them to be burnt to death.
    Full well the Inquisition might,
Such awful pow'r with his unite,
For well his harden'd heart they knew,
Philip had volunteer'd to view,
An " Act of faith," there to make known,
That all who Popish faith disown,
Should be condemn'd and doom'd to expire,
As heretics, in flames of fire.
    The day arrives, serene and clear,
The orient gleams of dawn appear.
The mountain tops of Spain are bright,
Gilded with rays of morning light.
From hills and groves the warblers raise,
Their lively, grateful hymns of praise,
Cheerful, since free to sit and sing,
Or fly abroad with out spread wing.
Not so with men, their faces wear,
An aspect gloomy, stern, severe,
For who, with cheerful heart, can go,
To witness scenes of human woe,
Though long taught bigotry should blind
His reason, or inure his mind,
To think that difference in faith,
Merits the punishment of death ?
    Anon the heavy, dull ton'd bell,
To take each victim from his cell,
The signal gives. Its solemn sound
To motion starts the people round.
From east and west, from south and north,
Men, women, children sally forth,

Eager, the pompous pageantry,·
And cruel spectacle to see.
Friars the grand procession lead,
To these the penitents succeed,
Close follow'd by an honest few,
Seceders, who no longer view
The Popish faith as sound, or true.
Next in the train, the firm, sincere,
Those who prefer all pains to bear,
Rather than suffer man to bind,
What is not man's, the faith, the mind.
Pictures to represent the fire,
In which the victims must expire,
With devils, on each one appear,
Painted in colors bright and clear,
Design'd the populace to show,
How heretics to hell must go.
Each has a Jesuit by his side,
True Pharisees in zeal and pride,
Adjuring him t' embrace the faith,
The Catholic, before his death.
Familiars and Inquisitors,
With num'rous other officers
Come next; then follows in the train
The grand Inquisitor of Spain,
Mounted upon a milk white steed,
Grooms by his side his horse to lead.
" And who is he," the crowd inquire,
" With lordly mein, and haughty air,
" Who seems above the rest to be,
" In splendor, rank and dignity ?"
" Tis Philip, 'tis the King of Spain,.
" Come the tribunal to sustain,
" Come to behold in flames of fire,.
" The stubborn heretics expire."
    The grave procession moves along,
Surrounded by the gazing throng,
To the great square, the field of death,
Where martyrs test, in fire, their faith.
An awful silence reigns around,

As they approach the savage ground.
Arriv'd, and all arrang'd, a prayer,
To give the act a pious air,
Is offered to the Lord to stay
The dreaded sin of heresy.
A sermon next is preach'd, to show
The Pope infallible and true,
And that the Inquisition must,
Because by him approv'd, be just.
"Behold your King, the pride of Spain,"
The Priest exclaims, "he will sustain
"Our holy faith, behold him here,
"His faith and purpose to declare."
    The King arises, swell'd with pride,
The sword suspended by his side
Unsheathes, and then proclaims aloud,
In presence of the assembled crowd,
"The holy Catholic faith I swear,
"Shall ever be my guardian care,
"The Inquisition while I reign,
"With all my pow'r will I maintain,
"Flames and the sword my realms shall free,
"From heretics and heresy."
    Thus Philip swears, then with delight,
Remains to view the savage sight.
    Posts firmly planted in the ground,
With dry combustibles around,
Exhibit to the victims' view,
The death they're doom'd to undergo.
But a kind voice, their souls to cheer,
A voice of love from Heaven they hear,
"Fear not my children, let the flames
"Burn and consume your mortal frames,
"Your Savior, your Redeemer's nigh,
"To Him your ransom'd souls shall fly,
"With Him forever to enjoy
"A bliss no tyrant can destroy."
The victims to the posts are bound,
While the vast multitude around,
Impatient wait the flames to see
    2*

Commence the burning tragedy.
" Beard them," the cruel people cry,
" Flames to their faces first apply."
The executioners their part,
Perform with skill, and practic'd art,
Raising with poles the glowing flames
To scorch their faces.   Loud acclaims
From the spectators rend the sky,
At this insulting cruelty,
While they, with fortitude sustain,
Unmov'd, the insult and the pain.
Slowly is fed the blazing fire,
That they, like slowly, may expire;
As if the pleasure of the scene,
Depended on the amount of pain,
And length of time it might extend,
Ere death their sufferings should end.
    Among the victims there was one,
A worthy, pious nobleman,
Who to the King he there beheld,
With soul undaunted thus appeal'd.
" Canst thou, O, King, such cruelty,
" Inflicted on thy subjects see ?
" What is our crime ?   An honest faith,
" For which we merit neither death,
" Nor punishment.   O, set us free,
" And we will faithful subjects be,
" As we have been."   The King declares,
In answer to the good man's pray'rs,
Who claims his mercy, " Should my Son
" The holy Cath'lic faith disown,
" Myself the fire would make with joy,
" That should the heretic destroy."
    Heaven heard and made the brief reply,
" By thine own hand thy Son shall die."
An awful sentence, justly due,
To such a rash, unfeeling vow.
    Unhappy Son, 'twas thine to hear
That awful speech, for thou wert there.
Unhappier still, thyself to find,

By his express command confin'd,
Abus'd, insulted, doom'd to bear
The pangs and tortures of despair,
'Till his inexorable wrath,
Procur'd the sentence for thy death,
Which from the Inquisition came,
That Father to absolve from blame.
    The sun below the western sky,
From this inhuman tragedy
Descended, night her curtain spread,
Before the martyrs' souls had fled,
From earth to Heaven, there to enjoy,
What human power cannot destroy,
Immortal life, eternal rest,
In mansions by their Savior blest.
    At length the tragic scene is past,
The blind, deluded people haste,
Each to his home, pleas'd to have been,
Spectators of the savage scene :
While King and Priests unite their power,
And Spanish freedom is no more.
No more his Spanish subjects sought
Freedom of action, or of thought.
Like slaves, in bondage bound, with awe,
They bow'd, submissive, to his law.
    Philip, triumphant thus, in Spain,
Like power determines to maintain,
In those free States his Sire resign'd,
To please his Son's all-grasping mind.
    The Netherlands, whose wide spread fame,
The world's deep gratitude may claim,
For their bold struggle, suff'rings, zeal,
Their rights against this tyrant's will
To guard.   This country, rich and free,
Renown'd for arts and industry,
And strong attachment to the right,
So odious in the bigot's sight,
The right to them, than life more dear,
The right, unaw'd, by force, or fear,
Of human laws, or human power,

Their God to worship and adore,
As should, in their belief, accord
With conscience and his holy word,
Yielding to Kings, what subjects owe,
The tribute for protection due.
   Philip beheld with jealous eye,
Their ardent love of liberty.
His haughty soul could not endure,
The least resistance to his power.
Hence he delay'd not to employ
The vilest weapons to destroy
Their freedom.   Art, deceit, disguise,
False promises and specious lies,
Awhile his warlike plans conceal'd.
At length his purpose was reveal'd,
By Edicts, which portray'd a mind,
Alike despotic and unkind,
A heart, too haughty and too hard,
Mercy, or justice, to regard.
" What were those edicts so severe ?"
You ask, most truly you shall hear.
   " Whoever shall, or hear, or teach,
" Or any other doctrines preach,
" But such as Popes and Priests ordain,
" Shall as vile heretics be slain.
" If women, they in earth shall lie,
" Buried alive, to mourn and die.
" If men, the sword, a milder death,
" Shall terminate their mortal breath.
" And whosoever shall deny,
" Or doubt the Pope's supremacy,
" Shall to the stake be bound, and there
" In slowly burning flames expire."
   These unjust edicts of the king,
Did war upon the people bring,
With all the horrors, all the woes,
Rage and intolerance could impose.
No mercy, that first Christian grace,
Found in his iron heart a place.
The Netherlanders saw that peace,

Or their religious rights must cease.
Indignant and resolv'd they rose,
Their rights to assert, his power oppose,
As best they might.   Meanwhile a host
Of Spaniards land upon their coast,
With Alva, cruel, skilful, base,
A demon with a human face,
For their Commander.   Mercy bleeds
To think of his inhuman deeds;
How blood and havoc mark'd the road,
The robber and his army trod ;
How men and women, old and young,
Were tortur'd, burnt, or drown'd. or hung ;
Or slain, by his ferocious band,
Hired t'enslave, or spoil the land :
How brave Count Egmont was betray'd,
To fraud most vile a victim made.
Egmont, whose noble deeds had prov'd,
He both his King and country lov'd.
His crime to Philip's mind was great,
Egmont had sought to save the State,
To heal dissensions, yet secure
To Philip all his lawful power.
His virtue was his crime, the spring
Whence rose the hatred of the King.
Egmont his country lov'd, his mind,
His heart, though Catholic, inclin'd,
To yield to Protestants the right,
So all important in their sight,
In their religion to be free,
From punishment for heresy.
For this, no former service done,
No new submission could atone.
His fate was scal'd, his death decreed,
Egmont, by Alva's hand, must bleed.
   Alva, to serve his master's end,
The Count solicits, as a friend,
To visit him.   The Count appears,
Feeling no guilt, he feels no fears.
Egmont, in Alva's power, too late,

Discerns the fraud, foresees his fate.
Seiz'd and secur'd by Alva's band,
His sword is wrested from his hand,
And he, by force, without delay,
Convey'd to prison, far away,
Far from his Province, far from home,
Where friends to save him might not come ;
In violation, clear and plain,
Of laws the King had sworn to maintain.
   Seized and secur'd, by such vile means,
No hope to save his life remains,
When tried by judges, all compos'd,
Of men, whom Alva knew, dispos'd
To find him guilty, men, indeed,
Who had, unheard, his death decreed.
   Thus perish'd, by a tyrant's hand,
The man who lov'd his native land,
The noble Egmont, honest, brave,
Who scorn'd, by crime, his life to save.
   The wily Alva was aware,
The people would not tamely bear
An act of perfidy so great,
So gross an insult to the State.
For this he car'd not, 'twas his aim
To wound their feelings, to inflame
Their anger, all their passions rouse,
Rashly his measures to oppose,
Then send around his secret spies,
Base, worthless wretches, in disguise,
To hear the people's speeches, see,
Who dar'd condemn his tyranny,
Then, without oath, or warrant, break
Into their dwellings, seize and take
The aged and the young, whose fate
Was death, too horrid to relate.
   The timid, thus, by force, or fraud,
By tortures, gibbets, overaw'd,
Abandon'd country, home and friends,
For liberty in other lands ;
Or staid, because too poor to go,

To witness other scenes of woe,
See cities sack'd, their brethren slain,
Their country pillag'd to maintain,
A rough, ferocious, foreign band
Of soldiers paid to scourge the land.
   Dark, dismal were thy prospects, long
The tyrant did the war prolong.
Yet thy great Statesman, unsubdued,
The power of Spain's proud King withstood.
Yes, William, Prince of Orange, thine
Was task most arduous, most divine.
'Twas thine, thy country's wrongs to feel,
To labor, with untiring zeal,
Her independence to maintain
Against this powerful King of Spain.
'Twas thine, with fortitude to bear,
Defeats and trials most severe,
Yet undismay'd, new efforts make,
Thy all upon the issue stake,
And thus the unequal war sustain,
And thus thy country's rights maintain,
Despite the fury of her foes,
'Till the bright star of freedom rose,
To give the land, despoil'd, opprest,
Peace, liberty, and needed rest.
   But, O, it was not thine to live,
Those well earn'd honors to receive,
Thy country had resolv'd to give.
No, the vindictive King of Spain,
Revengeful, as the murd'rer Cain,
Did, with malignant hatred, view
The Prince his power could not subdue;
Did, to appease his rankling rage,
His wounded pride and ire assuage,
By offers of a great reward,
Induce the infamous Gerard,
Thy life to take. This act so base,
So much to their, not thy, disgrace,
Committed by a wretch who feign'd,
To be thy follower and friend,

Came, like the lightning's flash, whose stroke,
Shivers, at once, the lofty oak.
Thus sudden was this great man's fall,
Shot at the door of his own hall,
Thus unexpected, was the blow,
That a whole nation fill'd with woe.
Tho' thus most infamously slain,
Thy deeds, on record, shall remain,
A living monument of praise,
More durable than art can raise.

No more of Philip, whose fell course,
No pangs of conscience, no remorse
Could check, we leave him, and his name,
A tyrant's, and a bigot's, fame.

A Queen, in those benighted times,
Of blood, and bigotry, and crimes,
Mary, the wife of Philip, reign'd
In England, and like him maintained,
Those slavish principles design'd,
First to degrade, then rule mankind.
Then England too, in flames of fire,
Suffer'd those good men to expire,
Rogers and Latimer, whose faith,
Surmounted all the pains of death,
With many more, compell'd to make
Like sacrifice, for conscience sake.

Turn next to France, and there behold
Intolerance like crimes unfold.
See Charles the ninth, with deadly rage,
Exterminating warfare wage
'Gainst Protestants, who claim'd to be,
In their religious worship free.
See him, as popish faith allows,
Assume the right to break his vows,
The right, deception to employ,
Or force, such subjects to destroy.

As Satan, when he tempted Eve,
The mask of friendship to deceive
Assum'd ; so Charles, with like intent,
The Protestants to circumvent,

Profess'd his subjects griefs to feel,
And strong desires express'd to heal
Dissensions, and to France, once more,
Peace and religious rights restore.
   The young Prince, Henry of Navarre,)
A Protestant, was doom'd to bear,   }
In this foul plot, a painful share.   )
This Prince, a youth of manly mind,
And soul to noble deeds inclin'd,
A treaty with the King had made,
Of fraud not dreaming, nor afraid,
His Sister to espouse ; the day
Of nuptials nam'd ; lively and gay
All Paris seem'd. The King with smiles,
With flatt'ring words, and crafty wiles,
The fears of Protestants allays,
Basely deceives and thus betrays.
   " Come, " said the King, to those good men,
Who had his faithful subjects been,
" Repair to Paris and unite
" To grace my Sister's nuptial rite.
" Let not our diff'rent creeds destroy
" Our future friendship, or the joy
" Your presence will afford."
Relying on his royal word
They came, were welcom'd and caress'd,
And oft the King his joy express'd
To see them there, and hop'd 'twould be,
A pledge of future harmony.
Too well the monarch play'd the part
Of traitor, with consummate art.
The Protestants, well pleas'd to find,
The King so gracious, lib'ral, kind,
Fearless within the City staid,
Not dreaming of the deep plot laid
For their destruction. Can it be,
Fiction, or faithful history,
The massacre we next unfold,
Which follow'd when the night bell toll'd ?
Not that glad bell which calls to rest,

3

The men with care and toil opprest.
No, 'twas the bell of death, the bell
To rouse those myrmidons of hell,
His popish partisans, who stood,
Thirsting for massacre and blood.
　O, 'twas a scene to make the heart,
With horror and amazement start.
Coligni first, whose honor'd name,
Stood high upon the roll of fame,
To whom his King and country ow'd
A lasting debt of gratitude,
Th' assassins sought, and forc'd their way,
Into the chamber where he lay.
Coligni rose and calmly stood,
Before the man who sought his blood,
And mildly said ; "Your aim I know,
" Nor can I shun the destin'd blow,
" Yet my gray hairs demand respect,
" Faith plighted, should my life protect,
" Yet strike, I know my destiny,
" I know 'tis order'd I must die."
A ruffian, answ'ring not a word,
Plunged to his heart the fatal sword.
Coligni fell.　With savage joy,
The cry went forth, " destroy, destroy,"
" Kill, kill," exclaim'd the monster King,
" The richest offering you can bring
" Our Mother Church, is blood of those,
" Who her authority oppose."
Swift at the words, the bigot crew,
Like light'ning, through the City flew.
" Death to all Protestants," they cry,
" This night the heretics shall die,
" This night our St. Bartholomew,
" No mercy shall blasphemers show."
　When two contending armies near,
For battle openly prepare,
It chills the blood within our veins,
We hear the groans, we feel the pains
Of dying men, we mourn, indeed,

That men on battle fields should bleed.
What then must be our feelings, when,
In secret conclave, murd'rous men,
A deep laid plot, a fatal snare,
To massacre their guests prepare ?
That night the unsuspecting wife
Beheld the dark assassins' knife,
Plung'd in her husband's heart, her child
Torn from her breast, affrighted, wild,
And murder'd.—Child and husband slain,
To plead for life she knew were vain,
Nor in that moment of despair,
Did she regret their fate to share.
That night, nor sex, nor rank, nor age,
From infants to the gray bair'd sage,
Found mercy.   The ferocious fiends,
Who call'd them there, as guests and friends,
Now rush'd upon them, unaware,
That danger, much less death, was near.
Thus unprepar'd to meet the blow,
Aim'd by a false, remorseless foe,
They fell, that night, like flocks of sheep,
When wolves into the sheep folds leap;
And faithful narratives have said,
The morning found ten thousand dead.
O, 'twas a sad, heart rending sight,
That awful morning brought to light.
Yet unrelenting papists could,
With triumph view that scene of blood,
Nay more, the bodies dead deface,
Thinking to death to add disgrace.
Nor was this horrid work of death,
This massacre for honest faith,
Confin'd to Paris.   Orders went
From Charles, by secret agents sent,
To all the Provinces, to rise
Forthwith, and murder by surprise,
The Protestants, who there might be,
Reposing in security.
Inflam'd with fierce, insensate zeal,

The tyrants orders to fulfil,
The papists rise, and sad to tell,
Full fifty thousand martyrs fell
In France, the King and Court to please,
And popish bigotry appease.
And yet for such vile treachery,
For such cold blooded villany,
The See of Rome to God did raise
Her impious thanks and songs of praise.
   In later times, like power and might
Have trampled on the sacred right
Of men, the word of God to read,
And form their own religious creed;
And persecutions, like a flood,
Have delug'd earth with crime and blood,
The spirit of reform to break,
And men the tools of tyrants make.
But painful, painful 'tis to trace,
These blood stain'd records of our race,
Nor do I, save the truth t' expose,
Religion rescue from the foes,
Who use it, as a cloak to hide,
Ambition, avarice and pride.
   O blessed Jesus, what a shame,
Men should invoke thy holy name,
Such crimes to excuse, and justify,
Intolerance and cruelty.
   Yet such was Popish bigotry,
No more akin to piety,
Than love to hatred, or the light
Of noonday sun to darkest night.
   Think not for Protestants we claim,
Exemption from their share of blame,
For acts of bigotry like base,
As those which popery disgrace.
Think not we purpose to applaud,
A Henry, Woolsey, or a Laud,
Or any, who like them would reign,
And power o'er faith by force maintain.
No, 'tis the spirit that would bind,

The faith and freedom of the mind,
The haughty, heartless, fiery zeal,
That seeks its own, not others weal,
That we condemn, wherever found,
On Protestant, or Popish ground.

THE SABBATH.

PART II.

When Popes and Priests, devoid of grace,
Could thus Christianity debase,
Could thus assume the right to bind,
The faith and conscience of mankind,
And Kings such measures vile employ,
Their subjects' freedom to destroy;
Why marvel, if long stifled ire,
Should burst forth, like the pent up fire,
Of a Volcano? Why expect,
Mankind should long such claims respect?
That infidels, ambitious, bold,
By no religious ties control'd,
Should not abound? Whose aim would be,
Not from such crimes the world to free,
Not the religion, strict and pure,
Of man's Redeemer to restore;
But men to leave, through life to stray,
No light divine to guide their way,
No God to serve, no souls to save,
No hope of bliss beyond the grave.
Such were the men, who since in France,
Their aims ambitious to advance,
No efforts spar'd to undermine,
All social truths, all truths divine.
The vices of the Priests they made,
Against Christianity to plead,
The people to corrupt, prepare,
For scenes of violence and war.
These men, the terror of their times,
Rose in proportion to their crimes;

The moral atmosphere became,
Charg'd with fit poison to inflame
The reckless, restless mass to hate
All that was good in Church, or State.
　Freedom, that precious gift of God,
When rightly priz'd, and understood,
The leaders made their constant theme,
Their stepping stone to power supreme.
'Twas not that freedom, just and pure,
Which virtue only can secure,
Nor that which would the nation bless,
With true, substantial happiness,
Which their deceitful tongues inspir'd,
And with feign'd love of country fir'd.
To govern France, in freedom's name,
With power despotic, was their aim.
Hence the false doctrines which they taught,
With ruin were, not safety fraught;
Doctrines, which spread o'er France a flood,
Of terror, anarchy and blood,
Rolling their guilt polluting waves,
To ev'ry land the ocean laves.
　These men inflam'd with lust and pride,
The being of a God denied,
Proscrib'd the Sabbath day, and made
An atheistical decade,
Follow'd by impious acts of shame,
Acts too indecorous to name.
　Mark the result, the issue learn,
The government of God discern.
" Let them alone," the Almighty said,
" Let them in their own ways proceed,
" Let them, like devils, proud and vain,
" Strive without God, on earth to reign,
" Let them blaspheme, and rave and rage,
" In the mad race for power engage,
" Trample on all, by fraud or force,
" The laws that should resist their **course** ;
" Destruction will their steps attend,
" Disgrace and ruin be their **end.**"

And now behold the conflicts dire,
Which envy, hatred, lust inspire,
'Twixt those, who rais'd the storm, to see,
Who should the chief director be.
See tyrants after tyrants bleed,
That other tyrants may succeed,
And thousands and ten thousands die,
Victims of rival jealousy,
Till one great master tyrant rose,
Who silenc'd all contending foes,
Who made all France his will obey,
Adjacent kingdoms own his sway,
Their kings solicit peace, and take
Such terms as he was pleas'd to make ;
Who, in his quenchless thirst for power,
From Rome, the aged Pontiff tore,
And him, by force, a pris'ner held,
Because to him, he would not yield,
His right of empire, nor resign
An office claim'd by right divine.
Napoleon thus, by fraud or force,)
Crush'd all he could, without remorse, }
Who dar'd resist his frightful course.)
And, as the miser, when his store,
Of wealth increases, covets more,
So, as Napoleon's power increas'd,
Did rage for more possess his breast,
Till the mad wish the world to rule,
Form'd the fix'd purpose of his soul.
Immense his efforts, but how vain,
The empire of the world to gain.
What though his bright and blazing star,
Led him to wage successful war ?
What though his arms in Italy,
In Austria, Prussia, Germany,
In Holland, Switzerland and Spain,
Did sudden, splendid conquests gain ?
All were not conquer'd, unsubdued,
An independent Island stood,
Like Atlas, to defy his rage,

The rock, the bulwark of the age.
And Russia, like a giant rose,
His last great onset to oppose.
Tremendous conflicts, deadly strife,
With loss immense of human life,
Ensued.   The world alarm'd, amaz'd,
With terror on the conflict gazed.
Russia enraged, his power defied,
Resolv'd his onset to abide,
Resolv'd his legions should retire,
Or on her soil disgrac'd expire.
    Nobly she stood, his fury brav'd,
Till Moscow's flames her empire sav'd,
Forc'd him reluctant to retreat,
By obstacles and perils great
Surrounded.   All around him rose,
Hosts of incens'd, avenging foes,
Impatient to harrass, annoy,
Impede, surprise, attack, destroy
His troops, scarce able to withstand
The storms that beat upon the land.
Such was the struggle, such the strife,
Among his flying troops, for life,
While plunging through the drifting snow,
Surrounded by a watchful foe,
That each his safety to secure,
Cared not what others might endure,
But fought, like hungry dogs, for meat,
Which none but starving men could eat.
Thousands from cold and lack of food,
Who fell exhausted on the road,
Were there, unheeded, left to die,
And, save in snow, unburied lie,
While obstacles increasing rose,
His troops, disheartened, to oppose.
    To save the remnant of his host,
The Beresina must be cross'd.
Thither, in miserable plight,
The troops direct their tardy flight,
Through forests, swamps, and fields of snow,
Pursued by their invet'rate foe.

Confusion, terror, and dismay,
Scatter the troops, their flight delay.
Weary, but driven by despair,
The stragglers to the stream repair.
Disorder follows, mass on mass
Rush madly on, in hopes to pass
The fatal stream.   A bridge, in haste,
Is o'er the freezing river cast.
And now begins the deadly strife,
The rush, the push, the strain for life.
  But soon a loud, heart-rending cry,
A scream of mortal agony
Is heard.   " The bridge, the bridge breaks down '
" See, see, it sinks, all, all is gone."
Loud lamentations, curses, sighs,
Of anguish and despair arise,
From officers and men, who see)
No end to their calamity,   }
But death, or dire captivity ;   )
For on their flanks, and on their rear,
The Russian troops are thund'ring near,
And thick their balls and bullets fly,
As hail stones from an angry sky.
  Here first Napoleon was known,
In bitterness of soul to own,
The sad, the lamentable fate,
That must his flying troops await.
  Himself to save, at dead of night,
Dressed in disguise, he takes his flight,
Abandons all, and hastes away,
Urging his flight by night and day.
  Alas, ill-fated men, opprest,
With famine, toil, and want of rest,
What could ye do, but suffer, die,
And there unmourned, unburied lie ?
And thirty thousand there, 'tis said,
That day were number'd with the dead,
Slain, and left freezing on the ground,
Or fleeing, in the river drowned.
  And thus this terrible campaign,

To conquer, and o'er Russia reign,
Was ended.   Buonaparte no more,
Could boast unconquerable power,
Nor rise from this tremendous blow,
This signal for his overthrow.
Great were his efforts to sustain
His sinking fortunes, but in vain.
The terror of his name was gone,
The spell that often led him on
To victory.   Hence came defeat,
And rapid, ruinous retreat,
As those disastrous battles show,
At Leipzic fought, and Waterloo.
　　Close press'd by foes on every side,
He struggles hard to stem the tide
That bears him down, too proud to yield,
Too proud to quit the battle field,
Till forced his throne to abdicate,
And yield, reluctant, to his fate.
" And must I then thus powerless fall ?
" Must I, who thought to conquer all,
" Who thought to make the world my own,
" Myself be conquer'd, overthrown ?"
　　Yes, thou who laid the nations waste,
Thyself the cup of woe must taste.
Thou who didst plunder, murder, lie,
The wrath of God and man defy,
To conquer and enslave the world,
Must from thy giddy height be hurl'd,
On a lone Island of the sea,
Thyself for life a prison'r be,
There to repine, lament, deplore,
The loss of thy ill-gotten power,
There, like a madman, in a cage,
Thy passions vent in fruitless rage,
There die, an outlaw, for thy crimes,
Mankind to teach, in after times,
That he, who seeks to conquer all,
Like mad Napoleon must fall.
　　Such were the men, who seem'd design'd,

This solemn truth to teach mankind,
That freedom is a plant too pure,
Of growth too holy to endure,
A soil, where irreligion spreads,
And nourishes its poisonous weeds,
With human blood.   Nations as well,
Might freedom hope to find in hell.
　　But why of bigotry complain,
Or infidelity arraign ?
Each with the self same ends in view,
Their own, not others good, pursue.
Self love, uncheck'd by justice, leads
Each to the like atrocious deeds.
In each the same proud spirit dwells,
Which all true Christian love repels,
For true Christianity is love
To men on earth and God above.
'Tis this which makes a nation free,
Man reconciles to Deity,
'Tis this which breaks oppression's chains,
And peace, with liberty, maintains.
　　And what but Christian love can bind,
What curb the passions of mankind ?
Sandbanks as well might floods restrain,
From sweeping o'er the adjacent plain,
Earth might as well with life abound,
And vegetation clothe the ground,
Should the great orb of day retreat,
And leave it neither light nor heat,
As pure religion be preserv'd,
Unless the Sabbath be observ'd.
　　But why should man from work abstain,
From worldly cares and thoughts refrain,
Each Sabbath day ?   Is he not free ?
Has he not power and liberty,
To manage, as his thoughts suggest,
His own affairs as he thinks best ?
Indeed, vain man, thou hast, 'tis true,
The power to will, to think, to do,
But 'tis a power thou must allow,

Thou didst not on thyself bestow.
Whence came thy life, thy reason, sense ?
Are they uncaus'd, the effect of chance ?
Chance has no object, no design,
No powers, no faculties divine.
Chance never made a watch, or clock,
Or key to fit the simplest lock,
Chance never made the flowing sail,
Or trim'd it to the rising gale,
Or ships to traverse oceans wide,
And o'er its waters safely ride ;
Nor aught that in his " march of mind,"
Man has completed, or design'd.
Much less, then, man, whose form divine,
Doth such superior powers combine.
View him in childhood, you will find
The germ of a progressive mind,
Quick to observe, compare, inquire,
Knowledge, by slow degrees, acquire,
From small, contracted objects rise,
To read the globes that deck the skies,
Their size compute, their motions trace,
Their circuits in the realms of space.
And did blind chance this globe prepare,
Suspend it safely in the air,
With sun to give it heat and light,
With moon and stars to shine by night,
And man a living soul create,
With body perfect and complete,
Fitted on earth as Lord to reign,
And his dominion there maintain ?
Who but a fool will dare advance,
That works like these are works of chance ?
Man is, indeed, a mystery,
His origin, his destiny,
Who can declare ? Shall finite man,
Almighty power and wisdom scan ?
What though he cannot comprehend, }
The works of an Almighty hand ? }
Shall he for this, unwise, contend ? }

There is no God, no Power Supremé,
That all religion is a dream ?
The universe a broad expanse,
Where order reigns, but reigns by chance ?
  If to the book of nature blind,
Your Maker there you cannot find,
Turn to the book reveal'd, there see
The true, the living Deity,
The world's Creator and your own,
The universal God made known.
Read well that book, learn how of old,
Moses, inspir'd of God, foretold,
What awful judgments, what disgrace,
Should fall on Israel's chosen race,
Whom he, upheld by God's command,
From Egypt to the promis'd land,
Through trying perils led, should they
Their Lord's commandments disobey.
Behold them, after forty years
Of trials, murm'rings, doubts and fears,
Of famine, war and pestilence,
Led through a dreary wilderness,
And settled by divine command,
In that delightful, fertile land,
Which God to faithful Abra'am's seed,
For their inheritance decreed,
That he, in them, a nation pure,
From idol worship might secure ;
A nation to record his name,
The Lord of Hosts, the great "I AM,"
The God, who made the heavens and earth,
The God, who gave all beings birth,
Whose laws support, uphold, control,
Direct and harmonize the whole.
And could the nation, thus redeem'd,
Thus for their Father's faith esteem'd,
Refuse his warning voice to hear,
And not His threaten'd judgments fear ?
Could they, unmindful of their Lord,
Neglect his worship and his word ?

And senseless, stupid homage pay
To idol gods, mere wood and clay ?
Yielding to all the mean desires,
Which lust inordinate inspires ?
  Yes, sinful nation, vain and proud,
Thy sins for vengeance call'd aloud,
By these provok'd, the Lord thy God,
Did stretch forth his avenging rod,
Stir up against thy guilty land,
A mighty Babylonian band,
Vassals of that proud King who rul'd
O'er many nations, uncontrol'd
By human power ; to whom was given,
By Him, who governs earth and Heaven,
A tyrant's lust, thy wealth to seize,
His proud, all grasping heart to please,
And to the splendor of his reign,
By conquest add thy rich domain.
  Not all thy efforts could withstand
This scourger of thy Father's land,
Whom God, for thy ingratitude,
And foul idolatries, allow'd
To enter, pillage, and destroy
Jerusalem, thy pride and joy ;
Thy temple built by David's son,
The wise, the far fam'd Solomon,
With sacrilegious hands t' explore,
Search for, and seize the golden store
Of vessels plac'd therein, for the use,
And service of that sacred house ;
And, with ferocious fury fir'd,
That temple, all the world admir'd,
To ashes burn, and strew the ground,
With ruins of the buildings round.
  Well might the Prophet weep and mourn,
For Zion of her glory shorn.
Well might his tears in torrents flow,
Well might his heart be fill'd with woe,
To see the City trodden down,
Her strong foundations overthrown,

Her young men and her virgins too,
To Babylon compell'd to go,
And nations more remote to toil,
Like slaves despis'd, on foreign soil;
Her people scatter'd far and wide,
In heathen nations to reside,
Subjected to perpetual fears,
Reproachful taunts and bitter sneers,
Compell'd to hear the Jewish name,
A by-word made, a mark of shame.
  Thus God, upon his chosen race,
Brought sorrow, bondage and disgrace,
Judgments most just for their neglect,
Her name and statutes to respect,
Judgments foretold, withheld, delay'd,
Till mercy could no longer plead,
Till all forbearance prov'd in vain,
Their sins, high handed, to restrain.
  But not, proud Babylon, to thee,
Was given this signal victory,
Save to chastise, a sinful, base,
Oft pardon'd, yet rebellious race.
Thou for thy sins, hast felt the rod,
The justice of a righteous God.
  O, that a seraph's coal of fire,
My lips would touch, my tongue inspire,
Of Babylon, the vain, the great,
The fall and the predicted fate,
And final ruin to relate.
That city, fortified around,
With gates of brass, and walls renown'd,
For height, and width and strength immense,
And proudly deem'd a sure defence,
Bulwarks impregnable, secure,
From all assaults of human power.
  But what can gates, orwalls avail,
When passions uncontrol'd prevail?
When pride, ambition, avarice,
And every base and kindred vice,
When men corrupt, seduce to sin,
  4*

Triumphant reign, those walls within?
Where kings and nobles, mad with pride,
The almighty King of kings deride,
Of molten gold an image make,
Which cannot hear, nor see, nor speak,
On Dura's broad, extensive plain,
With pomp erect it, and ordain,
That there the people all shall meet, ⎫
With reverence that image greet, ⎬
Fall down and worship at its feet? ⎭
Or with the grandeur of the State,
Its treasures, splendor, strength elate,
Unmindful of the Power supreme,
From whence their strength and treasures came,
They make their royal feasts and raise,
Their bacchanalian songs of praise,
To gods of silver, gold and brass,
By their own idol craftsmen cast?
    When creatures thus presume to be,
Creators of their Deity,
Shall not the Ruler of the skies,
The King of kings in vengeance rise?
Their revels change from mirth to woe,
Their impious kingdom overthrow.
Thus, by his Prophets, spake the Lord,
And with an oath confirm'd his word.
    " Great and exalted as thou art,
" Thy pride and glory shall depart,
" Thy wealth, the spoils of victory,
" And rapine, stain'd with cruelty,
" Like that which savage beasts of prey,
" On weaker animals display ;
" Thy City's vast magnificence,
" Guarded by gates and walls immense,
" Thy stolen treasures to secure
" From ev'ry foreign hostile power ;
" Thy temple of enormous size,
" With turrets towering to the skies,
" Erected not to Me whose name,
" Alone should adoration claim,

" But to a god of massive gold,
" To which your carnal hearts are sold,
" Gold which you worship and admire,
" As the chief object of desire,
" With all those wondrous works of art,
" Which beauty, grandeur, strength impart,
" To make thee great, shall, one and all,
" In everlasting ruins fall.
" A mingled mass, a mighty heap
" Of walls and buildings buried deep,
" Thy boasted City shall become,
" Nor ever more afford a home,
" A refuge, or a dwelling place,
" For any of the human race.
" E'en the wild Arab shall not dare,
" To pitch his tent, or harbor there,
" But o'er thy vast and proud domain,
" A horrid, death-like gloom shall reign,
" More dismal made by beasts of prey,
" By birds obscene that shun the day,
" And doleful creatures that reside,
" And revel 'mid those wrecks of pride,
" The only tenants of a land,
" Whose Kings did once the world command.
" Then shall all passers by exclaim,
" Is this great Babylon, the same,
" That conquer'd nations, Kings dethron'd,
" And them, as slaves, in bondage bound ?"
 And has not this great Babylon,
This glory of the kingdoms gone ?
Where now the vast magnificence,
The golden treasures, wealth immense
That fill'd the City ? Vanish'd, flown,
To victor foes and spoilers gone.
And where the hundred gates of brass,
Which unpermitted none could pass ?
Where the great palaces, the walls,
The spacious temples, festive halls,
And splendid domes erected round ?
Fil'd in vast ruins on the ground,

In mountain heaps, which passors by,
When they behold, astonish'd cry,
" Is this the mighty Babylon,
" The strongest City that the sun
" E'er shone upon ? Is this the fate
" Of that once proud, victorious State ?
" Lo, mid those desolations drear,
" Most horrid, frightful sounds we hear,
" From doleful birds, and beasts that sta
" Or prowl amid those wrecks for prey."
   Yes, passers by, you there behold
The wrecks of pride, so oft foretold,
There lie in wild confusion hurl'd,
Works once the wonder of the world,
This truth tremendous to declare,
That God the wicked will not spare.
   And where is Tyre, that splendid mart,
Of commerce, luxury and art ?
That grand emporium of the world,
Where num'rous ships their sails unfurl'd,
Spreading abroad her rich supplies
Of manufactur'd merchandise,
To interchange for products found,
In all the merchant ports around,
Thus daily adding to the store
Oo wealth she crav'd, yet craving more.
   Did not the Prophets of the Lord,
In graphic style her fate record ?
Declare that armies, like the waves
Of the vex'd sea, when roars and raves
The angry storm, in grand array
Should round her massy walls display,
Their hostile force,—that legions near,
With legions marching from the rear,
Should circle round her, and erect
Tents, mounts and batteries to protect
Their troops, and with huge engines break,
And breaches in her strong walls make;
With shouts of triumph, shouts of joy,
Her forts and garrisons destroy,

Soldiers and people slay, and seize
Her vast supplies of merchandize,
Her gold and silver, promis'd spoils,
And recompense for all their toils;
Her strong embankments overthrow,
That the great deep should overflow
The City, which, so long renown'd,
Though sought, should never more be found;
That fishermen their nets should spread,
Over the site where rest the dead,
The thousand and ten thousand slain,
Mingled with dust there to remain.

    Search well, ye sceptics, search, inquire,
Find, if you can, the once proud Tyre;
If not, be silent, nor deny,
What all inquirers verify,
That Tyre has fall'n, o'er her sweep,
The waters of the mighty deep.

    Again, ye sceptics, read, behold,)
How new discoveries unfold, }
The truths by ancient Seers foretold.)
Survey the land around mount Seir,
The prophecies against it hear.
Hear what the prophets of the Lord,
Commission'd to declare his word,
Denounc'd by his express command,
Against that Idumean land.

    " Thus saith the Lord, thy envy, spite,
" Thy exultation and delight,
" And clapping of thy hands to see,
" Jerusalem's calamity;
" Thy songs of triumph, shouts of joy,
" That cried, aha, aha, destroy destroy
" When by the King of Babylon,
" Her gates and walls were broken down,
" Shall be aveng'd on thine own land,
" On which I will stretch out mine hand,
" And make it desolate, lay waste
" Thy cities, cut off man and beast,
" Make desert all Idumea,

" Whose ruins shall perpetual be.
" Upon thy hills thy men shall die;
" Or, on thy plains, unburied lie.
" Thy ruin'd cities shall become, }
" For wild beasts that the deserts roam, }
" A hiding place, a transient home. }
" The bittern, vulture, cormorant,
" And raven shall their ruins haunt:
" There shall the great owl build her nest,
  The screech owl there find place to rest,
" And animals obscene and vile,
" The ruins that remain defile.
    " Yea, tho' in mountain clefts ye dwell,
" Possess the height of the high hill,
" Or in proud safety think to rest,
" High as the eagle builds her nest,
" There will I find thee, bring thee down,
" And make thy degradation known;
" Make thee to nations round a scorn,
" A wonderment to men unborn,
" Who may, in distant days, behold,
" The desolations thus foretold."
    Thanks to the spirit that inspires,
Late travellers with strong desires,
This land of wonders to explore,
Its state to learn in days of yore,
And from the ruins that remain,
Its former hist'ry ascertain.
    And what have these inquirers found,
On this denounc'd, accursed ground,
But desolations, wide spread waste,
Ruins and wrecks of ages past?
Memorials sad, from which to trace,
The fall foretold of Edom's race.
    Whence, but from God, could spring the light,
Which open'd to the Prophets' sight,
Such visions, terrible, but clear,
Of judgments, awful and severe,
That should in future, distant times,
Scourge Jews and Gentiles for their crimes?

Visions reveal'd, that men might know,
By evidence most strong, how true,
The oracles of God, how bright,
How overwhelming is the light,
Those oracles to all afford,
Who duly read what they record.
   In them we read of promis'd grace,
A Savior for the human race,
A Son from woman's seed to spring,
A Son to heal the serpent's sting,
The holy one of God, the same   )
The Prophets oft foretold, who came }
To glorify his Father's name,   )
The power of Satan to destroy,
And fill all earth and Heaven with joy.
   Search well the Scriptures, read, behold,
His birth, his life, his death foretold.
His Kingdom, that should stand secure,
Against the rage of human power;
His kingdom, built in righteousness.
Gentiles, as well as Jews, to bless;
Darkness from heathen lands remove,
Diffusing light, and life and love,
Where superstition long had reign'd,
And gross idolatry maintain'd
Its horrid rites, and bow'd men down,
To worship gods of wood and stone.
   The hist'ry of the world survey,
Before, and since that awful day,
When Christ, the Lamb of God was tried,
Nail'd to the cross and crucified.
Does not the period of his birth,
His life and ministry on earth,
His sufferings and death agree,
Strictly with ancient prophecy?
Has not his Gospel widely spread?
Has it not bruis'd the serpent's head?
And do not Christians, with delight,
Behold the spread of Gospel light,
With full assurance that the Lord,

Will bless the preaching of his word,
Until all nations shall be won,
To yield obedience to His Son.
  If then the Prophets were inspir'd,
What more of proof need be requir'd,
To prove that men are bound t' obey,
As God requires, the Sabbath day?
And what more needful, what more wise,
Could God in love to man devise,
Than bless for him one day in seven,
His thoughts to raise from earth to heaven?
  But if the Prophets you despise,
Deem their predictions forgeries,
Will you the Son of God reject?
His mission treat with disrespect?
With scorn, and hate, and proud disdain,
Mock, like the Jews, at Jesus slain?
Deny the miracles he wrought?
Dispute the doctrines that he taught?
Say the Evangelists all knew,
Their testimony was untrue?
Say the Apostles were deceiv'd,
And spake things not by them believ'd?
Say that his tomb was not unseal'd?
His resurrection not reveal'd?
Say 'twas deception, or a lie,
To which so many testify?
Dare you the character impeach,
Of Him who came the world to teach
Truths such as never man had taught,
Which light, and life immortal brought
To mortal men? Dare you deny
His wisdom, or his purity?
His love to man, than life more dear,
And yet believe Him insincere?
Believe the holy Jesus knew,
His claim to be "the Christ" untrue?
  By doubts and arguments like these,
Can you your consciences appease?
Examine well what Jesus taught,

His acts, with love and mercy fraught.
Think on the hopes sublime he gave
Of life and joy beyond the grave,
To sinners who repent, embrace,
With hearts sincere, his proffer'd grace.
Think with what wisdom, patience, zeal,
He toil'd and suffer'd to reveal
His Heav'nly mission, and proclaim
Salvation in his Father's name,
Redemption to th' immortal soul
Of man, reclaim'd from sin's control.
Think of his death, a world to save,
His close confinement in the grave,
From which, as he foretold, he rose,
Triumphant over all his foes:
Then pause, before you suffer pride,
Love so transcendent, to deride.

What rebel heart ought not such love,
To meekness and repentance move?
What prodigal on earth be found,
Who will not listen to the sound,
Of that kind voice which bids him come,
Repentant to his Father's home?

But if you still reject "The Christ,"
His proffer'd love and grace resist;
How will you calm your anxious mind,
When this short life must be resign'd?
How, but by Christian hope and faith,
Assuage the bitter sting of death?

Be not deceiv'd. On what men sow, ⎫
Sure as the word of God is true,   ⎬
Depends their happiness, or woe.   ⎭

Why does the husbandman prepare,
And cultivate his fields with care?
Select and sow the seeds design'd,
To grow and reproduce their kind?
But from assurance that each field,
Will an abundant harvest yield?

When God form'd man of flesh and soul,

With these combin'd on earth to rule,
Subject to Him, He left him free,
Free to enjoy his liberty,
Free to pursue, for good, or ill,
His own, or his Creator's will,
Free, at his peril, to transgress,
And risk immortal happiness,
Free to his flesh and lusts to sow,
And reap corruption, death and woe,
Or to the spirit, and receive
A spirit's gift, a soul to live.
   Men to supply their wants must toil,
Clear off the wild growth from the soil,
For pastures where their flocks may feed,
For fields with fruitful grain to seed;
For gardens, where the fragrant rose,
And flowers of brilliant hues disclose
Their beauty, rang'd 'mid trees,
Plants, shrubs and vines the eye to please,
The table with rich fruits supply,
A grateful, healthful luxury,
Priz'd and esteem'd by all, whose taste,
Intemperance has not debas'd.
But various tools are needful found,
For those who cultivate the ground,
And those who fit what they produce,
For market, or domestic use.
Hence to invent, and then to make
Machines, the place of hands to take,
Or supersede, by force of steam,
The carriage, stage coach and the team,
For artists, full employment finds,
To use their hands, and tax their minds.
   As men increase, wants multiply,
Which skill and labor must supply.
Houses, with all their furniture,
Domestic comforts to secure;
Cities for trade, ships to transport
Rich merchandise from port to port,

Must all be built, renew'd, repair'd,
By toil of millions working hard.
To these, to all, how needed, blest,
How sweet should be a day of rest.
Like as the parch'd and thirsty plain,
Needs the refreshing shower of rain,
So men, with weekly toil opprest,
Need the refreshing power of rest.
Hence God, in mercy to mankind,
The Sabbath for that end design'd,
And bid them keep it.   And shall they
Their God and Father disobey ?
   Behold the village where you hear
No summons to the house of prayer,
No gathering of people see,
To worship on the Sabbath day.
A faithful picture of the place,   }
Presents a grov'ling, vicious, base,
Degraded, unenlighten'd race.
The tavern and rum-selling store,
The bane and ruin of the poor,
Stand prominent.   These idols there,
Tax their poor worshippers most dear,
For their delusion   Comfort, wealth,
Strength, moral dignity and health,
And talents too, which hand in hand,
Like plants well cultur'd, should expand,
Grow up, bud, blossom, bear
Fruits worthy of the cultor's care,
With all that elevate the mind,
Are to the idol rum resign'd.
   O, wretched men, will no desires,
Save what base appetite inspires,
Rouse you to break the spell that binds,
In bondage, your immortal minds ?
To stop the slow, consuming flame,
The fire that wastes the human frame,
Its strength destroys, its beauty mars,
And all its moral powers impairs ?

Vices, most sordid, will be found,
Where men, degraded thus, abound,
Of which a few mean sharpers take
Advantage for vile lucre's sake.
There you will see a magistrate,
With his commission from the State,
The peace to keep, offences try,
Riots, assaults and battery,
A Lawyer too, with small pretence,
To learning, or to common sense,
An Empyric, who boasts of skill,
Which practice proves, is good to kill.
These, with rum venders, rule the place,
Fill it with misery and disgrace,
And thus to live, the means procure,
By making all the others poor.
     Hence houses old, with rotten cells,
With clapboards loose, for want of nails,
With windows stuff'd with rags unclean,
Throughout the village will be seen,
And in each house be found a hell,
Where sickness, want and discord dwell.
     Does such a picture pain your mind?
Would you a brighter, fairer find?
Go where the people all unite,
To greet the Sabbath with delight;
Where old and young, with joy repair,
To worship in the house of prayer.
In that blest village you will see,
Order, combin'd with industry;
See in the bonds of Christian love,
All in their proper stations move;
See children, by their parents taught,
Lessons, with truth and wisdom fraught;
Lessons, which on their hearts impress,
The love, the worth of holiness:
And fit them, when of riper age,
In life's great duties to engage;
Like servants, faithful to fulfil,

With all their might, their master's will.

   Then, when their lease of life shall end,)
To Heaven their spirits shall ascend, }
An endless Sabbath there to spend ;)
A Sabbath of unmingled joy,
Which will their noblest powers employ,
Their views expand, their minds improve,
In knowledge, purity and love.

NOTE

In the facts alluded to in the foregoing poem, I have taken history for my guide, without attempting to heighten their interest by any fanciful exaggerations. Indeed, the persecutions of the Reformers, usually denominated Protestants, in the sixteenth century, by Philip II., King of Spain, Netherlands, &c.—by Mary, his wife, Queen of England, and by Charles IX., King of France, contemporaries, and intolerant Papists, are of a character too revolting to the feelings of humanity, for a detailed narration of all the horrid crimes and cruelties that attended them. I have, therefore, only adverted to some of the most prominent events of that awful period.

Those, who are unacquainted with, and who desire to know more of, the history of those persecutions, are referred to Watson's life of Philip II., Russell's Modern Europe, and the history of the Reformed Religion in France.

The horrors of the French revolution, and the all grasping ambition of Napoleon, to be the world's sovereign dictator, are recent events, with a knowledge of which but few are unacquainted. They are well narrated in Scott's life of Napoleon, and various other histories.

For information in regard to the prophecies contained in the Scriptures, and their subsequent fulfillment, to which allusion is made, as evidence of the truth of divine revelation, Keith on the Prophecies may be consulted.

Extracts from various writers were prepared, fully proving the truth of all the facts stated, but I have thought a general reference to some of them would be preferable, as they are in most of our Lyceum and Social Libraries, and may be readily consulted.

Printed by BoD™in Norderstedt, Germany